Somehow, Somehow

Somehow, Somehow

Written and illustrated by
Nyanda Foday

ANDERSEN PRESS

First published in 2024 by
Andersen Press Limited
20 Vauxhall Bridge Road, London SW1V 2SA, UK
Vijverlaan 48, 3062 HL Rotterdam, Nederland
www.andersenpress.co.uk

2 4 6 8 10 9 7 5 3 1

All rights reserved. No part of this publication
may be reproduced, stored in a retrieval system or
transmitted in any form, or by any means, electronic,
mechanical, photocopying, recording or otherwise,
without the written permission of the publisher.

The right of Nyanda Foday to be identified
as the author and illustrator of this work has
been asserted by her in accordance with the
Copyright, Designs and Patents Act, 1988.

Copyright © Nyanda Foday, 2024

British Library Cataloguing in Publication Data available.

ISBN 978 1 83913 503 3

Printed and bound in China

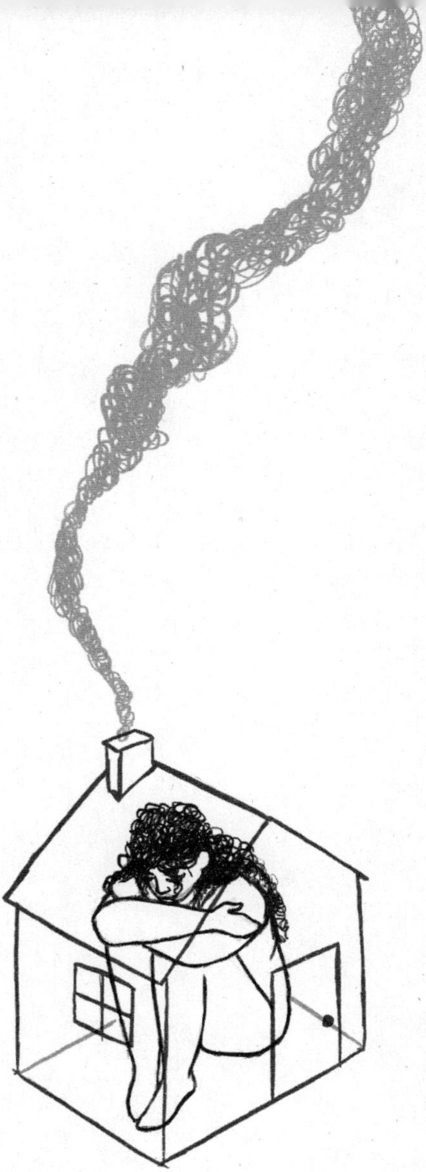

Contents

Conversation Topic	01	Help	31
Contamination OCD	02	Body	33
Alone (Part 1)	04	Sarah Everard (1987-2021)	35
8 O'Clock News	06		
Video Calling	08	Morning Walk	37
Empty Shelves	10	Student of the Pandemic	39
Applause	12		
Grocery Lines	14	My Little House	42
Hot Air	16	Family is Complicated	45
May 2020	17	Test Taking	48
Self-soothing	19	Groceries, Again	49
Quizzes	21	Poppy	52
Oracular	23	BLM	54
Alone (Part 2)	25	Creating	57
First Time Going Out	26	Post-pandemic	60
Return	28		
Time	29		

Conversation Topic

I am in a park with strangers
When it becomes something to talk about.
We laugh,
Stand a little apart.
The Prime Minister is suggesting herd immunity.
We make our plans for our project-
We don't know yet-
We say:
It should be fine,
So long as we remember to wash our hands

Contamination OCD

I am in a Nando's with my parents
When I realise that I cannot do this the way they can.
When I track my father back from the sink
And see everything he's touched
And want to rush back and wash again and again.
I don't have contamination OCD.
Yet.
My flavour is hoarding and intrusive thoughts
But I can feel the way my brain shifts,
Alert.
It says: Here is a new thing to be afraid of
It s almost not even about the germs
It says: If you're going to do it, do it right.
That's when I decide to stop going outside,
That's when I decide that it is better to have nothing,
Than play around with 'careful'.
I spent most of the pandemic more afraid of passing it
Than catching it-
I said: If I see nobody,
If I am locked away for all but two hours a week,

Please, please don't let me hurt anybody.
I gave it up
I gave it all up
I would do it again.

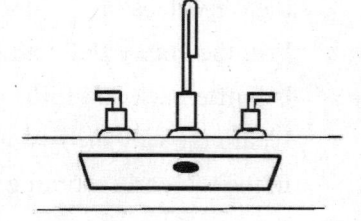

Alone (Part 1)

When my housemate tells me he's thinking about going home,
I tell him that I support whatever decision he needs to make.
And when he tells me he's going home, I hug him.
And my family is in Birmingham
And I am in Manchester, 75 miles away.
And I decide to stay.
The flat becomes my domain
I stretch the days out into vague spaces
Of shuffling back and forth
I create art
When I can.
I only leave the house once a week to get food
I stay inside
I am completely inside
I do not see anyone
I leave videos on
I fill the empty flat with the sounds of strangers talking
I shuffle back and forth
I learn the way the living room glows orange
In the too-early morning

I stop sleeping right
I learn that I love to be awake for a sunrise
I make every room my room
I take a nap in a sunbeam
I learn how to get by
I tell myself it will be okay
I dress for the mirror
I order in dinner
I let myself drift through the day
-The days-
I put my thoughts that are too loud
        for my head on Instagram
My friends and I do weekly videocalls
I create more art
I fill the flat with paintings
I make it through every day
Somehow, somehow
I do my exams
Somehow, somehow
I stay alone.

8 O'Clock News

I've never been one for the news
But this is a different type of update.
For the first time things seem to change by the day
So I lazily open a tab –
YouTube is streaming it live
His face turns my stomach
I swallow it
Watch it anyway
Wade through political sweet nothings
        I don't care about
I just want to know what's happening,
What's changing.
What are we doing?
Can we go outside?
What is a bubble?
How many people have died?

When it finishes, I find an article to double check
        what it all means
Send a message out to the group chat,

Restructure my perspective on what's coming
Traipse through my empty flat.

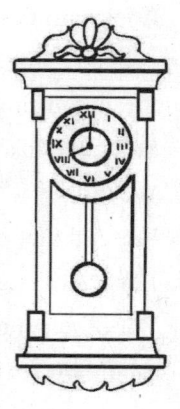

Video Calling

I don't like to start a Zoom call
Even though I am always ready first.
Preferably fifteen minutes before the agreed start time,
Just in time to watch the messages pour in:
I'll be there in a minute, just getting a drink.
Same.
When the call starts, I always forget to wait
          to join audio before speaking
I wave at people as they filter in
We re-remember how to start-stop-speak
Rundowns of our days
Look into the corners of people's bedrooms
          for things of note
Strange tilting as we are moved down to a kitchen
Someone has remembered that filters are a thing
We talk.
Pretend that we are not looking at ourselves half the time
For me, it is good enough,
For others, not so much.
And then we trail off.

Someone reluctantly brings up the idea of the end
        and we all stumble to join in-
No one wants to be the person being left, you see.
We say goodbye.
Decide if we are leaving the meeting or waiting
        for the host to end it
And suddenly you are staring at just a screen again,
And your house is silent.
And you're alone again,
So suddenly.
So you hop onto the group chat
'It was lovely to talk to you all, *heart emoji*'

Empty Shelves

In Asda I find
Empty shelves
And fear
And the urge to grab and stockpile
And the obsession with toilet paper
And milk
And bread
And yeast
And flour.
It's kind of funny? Now, at least-
These are the things we decide that
      we need in an emergency,
I guess.
On the day Asda brought back flour, all the kilo bags
      had already gone,
So I bought a five kilo bag for about a tenner.
I was Confident that I could get it back
My mother wanted me to call an Uber
But I wanted to be Covid safe
And it was a hot, sweaty summer

And I carried it home in probably less than five
        minute bursts– I lived close enough.
I brought my winnings back to my building
And halfway up the first three flights of stairs,
        my loud neighbour who played music
        at inconsiderate times, and smoked weed
        that curled its way into my bedroom at night,
        and was having people over in spite
        of Everything-
He offered to carry it up for me.
We didn't have a lift.
And I awkwardly thanked
And followed behind him,
And I had brought my spoils back to my home,
And like everyone else in the pandemic,
I made myself bread.

Applause

If you
Clap
Hard enough
It Might
Make up for
    The hours,
        The lack of protection,
            The budget cuts
And
If you
Smile
Hard enough
    At your neighbour
        (Whose name you
            never learned)
    It might make them someone you care about
And
If you
Do this
Every Week

       At 8 p.m.
It might be like a prayer
       Or something bigger
And
If you
Try hard enough
       You can pretend
       That there is community here
That we are all in this together
That this country cares about its 'essential workers'.

Grocery Lines

The Asda car park is directly in the sun
And a queue is winding itself around, so long
        it might be funny,
If I feel like laughing at it.
I'm listening to a podcast
And I have nowhere to be,
So,
I make my way to the back, calmly.
I'm good at waiting
-I suck at anticipation, but waiting is different
I like feeling like it's out of my control
That I've done my job
And all that's left to do
Is wait.

We serpentine steadily along the not-tarmac,
Following the bright yellow lines that weren't there
        a few months ago.

The first stage of pandemic, things moved so quickly
> but life turned slow.

I, who was only leaving my house once a week,
Relished in the feel of the sun on my face.
Let myself be warm,
Resting in one long moment.

Hot Air

The me in the video says,
'This is the first time I've spoken out loud today.'
She is living alone
And the walls have never asked for her thoughts.

When the world reopened
And when I finally stepped back out
I had lost about half my voice.
It still happens
An evening of chatting and I am hoarse
Something atrophied in the still
And I am holding a handful of words and trying
        to make them last
Trying to say something worth hearing.
I don't know that I'm managing
I miss the way I used to speak.

May 2020

The worst month of my life was May 2020
It was my second month of living alone
I had two big submissions a week.
Would drag my body from my bed to a table to write
        Something
Anything, whenever I could
Some days I just lay down
Some days I made beautiful art
A lot of the time I cried
Some days I didn't speak out loud
Even to myself
Some days I barely ate
Some days I was convinced I would fail.
May was a month of gritted teeth
Bare knuckling through
Listening to hours and hours of D&D actual plays to fill
        the room
Getting back into bed whenever I need to
Holding myself
However I needed to

Forgiving myself
For everything
For things that had nothing to do with me
Sending reassuring messages to whoever
        needed to hear them
Recording videos of me explaining and narrating and
        crying just to feel seen.
May was a month I survived more than anything
But I did,
And now it gets to just be a sentence,
And a thing I lived through,
And every year it becomes less real
And more story than anything else,
And I pile the new Mays on top of those memories
And I keep moving forward.

Self-soothing

In lockdown I start holding myself,
Arms clutched around my waist.
I murmur to myself:
It's okay you're okay we're okay.
I haven't been hugged in a very long time.
Repetitive motion is soothing
I stroke my hand down my own arm,
It feels better to keep moving
I clutch tighter
If you say it out loud enough times it becomes real:
It's okay
You're okay
We're okay
I take us to the living room,
I make us food,
I take us to bed,
I take us to the shower.
It's okay
You're okay
We're okay

It becomes a little truer
I move myself through the day
I do what I can,
I forgive myself for what I can't.
It's okay
A thumb down the outside of my arm
You're okay
Just as firm on the upstroke
We're okay.

Quizzes

This week we are doing quizzes on
      our weekly Zoom call.
It's kind of beautiful.
They are self-referential,
A group of friends who have known each other
      for three years
Finding new things to learn about.
One friend with a tendency to dissociate asks
      us questions without concrete answers
He asks to describe his perfect house,
Whether he is more like 25 or 36,
The colour of him,
And we all imagine together,
Tell stories to our friends about our friends and some
      imagined future.
I ask them which mythical creature I would be, and
      tell them that there are two correct answers.

There can be an urge to write purpose into tragedies
To tie up the plot points neatly

To say we suffered, but it was worth it because we
                learned or changed or grew or we're resilient now
Because we've done it before and we can do it again
Because there has to be something good to see
                in the horror of it all.
And now, years down the line, I can miss those quizzes
That intimacy
That eagerness to learn more about the people we love
But none of those moments of humanity were worth
Any of it, really.
Two things can simply have happened
And a tragedy is sometimes just tragic.

Oracular

When my flatmate and I video call a
        friend for the first time,
She points out a conversation we had,
Long before this all started.
Where we, in all our omniscience, had
        explained simply biology:
        That for all our human arrogance,
        Nature is unstoppable.
        That if we continued to grow and take
        and grow, nature would have to cull.
        We laid out the best possible
        circumstances for her-
        A disease,
        Indiscriminate,
        Cut back the population
        Nature will balance.
She tells us, jokingly, that we did this.
It's brushed off easily enough.

But it wasn't indiscriminate, was it?

And humans are far from their carrying capacity,
And much of this death wasn't a result of pure,
>	unfeeling biology
But policy
And greed.

Alone (Part 2)

He returns to me on the 79th day
And I cannot stop crying when I am finally held again.

First Time Going Out

It is summer and they have told me that the pandemic
>is over -

It isn't.
But my friend will be back in Manchester
>and I don't know if I can meet her

I don't know what it feels like to be outside around
>people again,

I need to know if I can say yes,
So my returned roommate leads me, knock-kneed,
>to a local park.

He kindly ignores the way I flinch when strangers
>get too close,

I am like a baby deer,
Wide eyed and uncertain
And the colours of the trees are so vividly green-
I think I lost some of my colour to the walls of my flat-
It's so vibrant out here,
And I don't know if I'm excited or scared.
A couple comes closer than I would like them to
I feel my spine stiffen

Everyone I look at is just
Living.

I want to be angry at them
I want to scream at all the people who somehow
        just pressed pause,
They are all so easily playing again—
I lost something.
I am shaking.
We don't sit down in the park
We keep moving.
It wasn't the kind of thing I could do, it was the
        kind of thing I had to move through –
We did one circuit and he led me back home again.
I didn't cry
I might as well have.
But I got to make plans to meet my friend

Return

I am the first to move in for the new semester.
I am used to the isolation at this point.
I pace out the unfamiliar space
Get stuck in an OCD loop for a day or two,
Get comfortable in my new room.
My housemates filter in slowly,
I get used to sounds that don't come from me
It is nice to hear someone else's laughter
           echoing through the halls
And the practising of musical instruments
Brass
Drifting down through the floor to my ceiling.
I am still separate from them – the only one
           who sleeps on the ground floor
But I am close to the kitchen
Our little hub of sorts
And I am not alone any more.

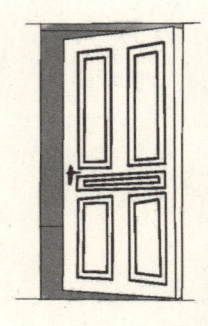

Time

The pandemic is in a toxic relationship with the
        passing of time
Stuck somewhere between clinging and rejecting.
No one knows the difference between hours
        or days or weeks or months any more
There is a fingerprint smudge through my calendar
I am watching time drip through the boxes
Mixed into indecipherable sludge-
The thing about remote work is
I can do it whenever
Actually.
Half a year into a pandemic and my body has forgotten
        its circadian rhythm
One of my housemates, I no longer see – there is no
        overlap in when we are awake any more
I am spilling slowly over into nocturnal,
None of it matters anyway,
I can do anything at any time so long as it is done
        and I am at home
I am always at home,

I use the night to pretend I am alone
A girl gets used to her space after so much of it, after all
And I don't know how long it's been since I've seen
      my mother/father/brother/grandparents/friends
And no one knows how long this will last
And time continues to drip and shift
      and spill through our hands.

Help

The lecturer sends an email to us all.
He says:
Times are tough
And I
Am understanding –
Compassionate.
If you need anything,
Let me know
And I will help.

So I confess.

Word after word of it all
Expose
Self-flagellate
Here, sir, are all the things wrong with me,
        I'm so glad you're finally listening.
It's hard.
Did you know how hard it is?
I barely leave my bed, sir.

I'm trying
But it hurts, sir
Thank you for trying back -

His reply
Is something along the lines
of
I'm sorry.
I didn't mean it like that-
It's more than I meant
You're too broken to help
I recommend the service you've been through
        three times instead –

I sigh
I don't reply
I sew up all the wounds I reopened for him.

Body

Everyone's talking about their pandemic weight.
Laughing, pained.
Trying to pretend they're fine with it on the best days,
Grimly muttering about how they're going
        to get rid of it on their worst.
I loved mine more.
In not being seen I was finally able to feel-
To feel the way the curve of my side
   fits my hand perfectly
To finally be able to rest my hand on my stomach
And instead of fearing the way it looks,
        to feel the reassuring weight
To be calmed by it
To get to know myself again with no worry of aesthetic
To wear a long T-shirt with no bra every day with
        no thought of what someone else might see
In the isolation I returned to nudity
My body
Became
Safe again

In a way it hadn't been in a very long time.
No one to comment on it
No one to apologise to for it
I could just exist,
In the neutrality of it all
Refamiliarise myself with it
Take as much space as I need
I do not know if I gained weight over the pandemic,
Though I suspect it.
I do not care.
With no one else to hold, I held myself
Came home to myself.
For the first time in a long time,
I let my body be.

Sarah Everard (1987-2021)

When the police officers assaulted women at the vigil
And I shared my disgust
An old friend popped up.
He pointed out that it wasn't sexism, it was just . . .
        Covid compliance
And the family didn't want the vigil anyway.
I responded, strongly worded
But there were things I didn't say.
I didn't tell him how many friends I had watched
        unfold stories on the kitchen table
I didn't tell him about the girl that came
        to stay in our flat in first year that night
        because her room was a crime scene
Or the way I held the friend hosting her as she cried
And I didn't tell him about how long it took my friend
        to admit to herself what had happened to her
And I didn't tell him about the lecturer messaging
        my coursemate to tell her how pretty she was

And I didn't tell him about the week I couldn't
>   leave the house without a man yelling at
>   me, touching me, insisting on my attention
I didn't explain how it feels when a man on a bike
>   rides up next to you when you know
>   you're about to arrive at your house and you
>   don't know what the safest course of action is.

He was supposed to be safe.
And he wasn't.
And she was supposed to be safe.
And she wasn't.
And her loss was a Tragedy.
But anyone who thought it was just about what
>   happened to one woman wasn't listening.

Morning Walk

My housemate has started taking herself
        on walks in the morning,
A faux commute before a long day of working
        in her bedroom.
Sometimes I join her –
A way for her to start the day, a way for me to end mine.
8 a.m. looks different from this side.
We walk to the park, spotting small houses along the way
        and imagining how happy we could be
        in a place like that.
Mapping out futures that are hard to believe in
        after a year of change and uncertainty.
We shake them off,
We follow the path,
I pluck flowers off a tree
I will take them home
Try to press them between the pages of a textbook
        I don't use
Just to keep something beautiful.
She thinks it's sweet.

We breathe,
Enjoy the air
The space
The moment.

Student of the Pandemic

I fall into bed like a ragdoll.
All my strings cut and my bones pressed to a paper
        I should have been writing notes on
I don't know how to go on,
These days I am sitting in my bed all day
Same place same way
Until my arse starts to sting and I slump.
I've been in a slump for some time now
I don't really care about my education any more and all
        I had had up to this point was that
        vague academic goal and now my
        new reality is sitting staring at a screen
        and wondering if I'll ever get my degree.
And wondering if I still care about my degree.
As I reach out to my supervisor the second time this week
She is scattered.
I want to yell at her that she is the only tether I have
        to my university

I have no lectures or seminars or groups
I am nothing but a face on her screen
£9,250 to not step on campus
Times 4
£37,000 to give up at the last moment
I don't know what I was paying for.
The head of my undergrad experience told me
    that I could maybe have that extension if
    I could prove that my depression
    was made worse by pandemic and family
    deterioration
She asked for evidence after I said that I had none
She told me she would be in touch and then she wasn't
I am tired of chasing up people who are too busy
    and underpaid to help me
My university told us to think of lockdown as a retreat,
Denied mitigating circumstances to a boy
    in hospital hooked up to an IV.
The only thing tethering me to reality is an institution
    that can't even give me apologies
No wonder I want to drift
No wonder I need to sleep
No wonder all I do is sleep

As all the work I should be doing piles up and the
    people I should be hearing from are nowhere
    to be seen
And I still have to keep going
Because all I am now is the walking debt
And there are no opportunities on the horizon.
I wanted to do a PhD
Now I just want to sleep.
I work for an hour a day a few days a week
And then I sleep.
This corner of my bed makes up the four walls
    of my reality
And the university has sent me another fucking
    wellbeing email where they recommend
    mindfulness, water, and taking regular breaks.

My Little House

Living by myself was the hardest thing I had ever done,
And it wasn't so much a choice I chose as the place
        I found myself.
One might think that in the aftermath
        I would cling to others-
Fill my home with bodies and people and presences.
Before the pandemic I would have sworn that I couldn't
        do it alone,
But I did.
And now I do.

In the uncomfortable, misshapen space between
        higher education and becoming a full
        person, I found myself in a two-bed
Choking on my own privilege as I eagerly drank it down
-I still haven't worked out how to sit with it.
It is my little space
Where no one is allowed in unless I invite them.

In the 8 long months that followed in long, shameful
>   unemployment, I reshaped it into a safe haven.

My dog moved in.

I hold her,

Take her to the park,

Let my dishes pile up when they need to

Waste a weekend when I need to

No one knows how long it's taken me to wash my sheets.

I carve out space to be me

I order deliveries and buy ready meals to make sure I eat

I crawl back into bed when I need to

I make space for myself

I let myself strive for less

I watch the things I love

I make art that I find beautiful

I forgive myself.

Again, and again

I forgive myself for all the things I cannot do

I am radical in my acceptance of mediocrity and failure

My degree lives in a drawer

I leave it there

I let myself just live

I write poems just for me

I let myself write bad poetry
I don't dress most days
I let myself feel ugly
I decide being ugly is okay,
When people visit, they tell me that my home is calm
I tell them it is on purpose.
People come to my home to do nothing
        and I find that beautiful.

I do not own this house and I do not know
        that I will ever own a house
But while I am here I own this space Fully
And I feel Safe again.

Family is Complicated

I lost my relationship with my father over the pandemic.
It feels dramatic to say it
It's something I've only just started saying out loud,
      I suppose.

It was a strange time to do it.
When I was in Manchester and everyone else all lived
      together in Birmingham.
And we didn't see each other-
Couldn't
I almost didn't go home for Christmas,
So he went to stay with his sister,
And I felt guilty.
Like I had shunted him out of a structure
Like I Had to go home now,
Because he had taken that sacrifice out of my hands
And worn it so well,
Ever the martyr.

It wasn't an explosive separation-

I don't know that we ever yelled once at each other.
And in the pandemic, you just get used to not seeing people
I guess
I think.

There was so much talk around losing people,
But not like this.

I don't remember the last time we talked.

I wonder if things would have gone differently
        if he had been able to drive up and see me
          (I didn't want him to)
If he hadn't been trapped in a house with the rest of my family
If the phone call that started it would even have happened
        if I could have come home for the weekend
          (I don't think I would have)

I think things might have been different
In another version
Maybe.
But this is the one I live in
And it sits wrong under my skin

And that has to be fine
Because that's just the way it is

Test Taking

I read the instructions every time
Just in case
Push the cotton swab up just a little further,
        because I do not know how deep 2.5 cm is.
And my kitchen counter is a laboratory
Items laid out in perfect precision
I wonder if I am squeezing hard enough
Or too hard
I enjoy placing the drops, despite myself
And as I wait I package all the waste away
A biohazard in my own home.
I try not to look early
Just in case
Just in case
Cross a single pink line through my fears.

Groceries, Again

I don't shop like I used to.
I don't remember how I used to shop, of course-
Acts of mundanity are rarely something we
        bother to keep preserved in our memory-
But I know it wasn't like this.
I'm a little better, obviously
But it's still
Wrong.
I put on my mask as I enter
Get my basket
Begin to track the same tread around
I get the same things,
I don't deviate,
I know what works
I feel my presence slipping-
I'll just get the same things
-The hum of distant alarm starts buzzing under my skin.

I know I never used to shop like this.
In a dissociative haze as I panic-

I can come Back if I need to
              But my brain doesn't understand that
I am haunting the aisles,
To anyone else my face is just wide eyes,
I am just putting things in on autopilot

I panic grab two things
How much is anything?
Cost of living

I am at the tills
Thanking everything in me that they have installed
              a self checkout.
As I scan the items through I try and work out if
              I have enough to feed myself for a week
I don't know
I don't know
I don't think so?
I don't know.

I accept it.
Leave with my yellow reusable shopping bag.
I hate the colour yellow

And the feeling of the straps digging into my hands.
I relish in the feel of taking the mask off as I leave the shop
I can breathe again
I don't know if it's helping anything,
    but I think it's the right thing?
I don't really know any more.
I make it home, unpack,
Pretend I won't have to do it again next week.

Poppy

When I say that I think my dog saved my life
I don't mean it in a dramatic way.
I don't mean it with the severity of circumstance
        that I'm sure is assumed.
I mean it in insignificant, everyday ways.
That she gave me a reason to get up regularly,
In the morning, specifically
– Even if I got back into bed as soon as she was fed.
That I had to put clothes on to take her out.
I would sit in the green as she ferreted through
        underbrush and chased senses far beyond me.
I remembered that, for all my indoor kid energy,
I love trees.
I would write out there, and I still do.
She gave me a reason to speak out loud,
Most days were filled with declarations of adoration,
        of love.
Having someone to hug.
Having someone to call in the middle of the night
To sob into her fur.

I might well be an old dog lady in the making,
I am unapologetic.
When I say I think my dog might have saved my life,
    it is not some trite soundbite
And not a day goes by where I don't worry about the
    undeniable fact that she will not be here forever
That she is already old, for a dog
And has given me more love than
    I can begin to express,
But while I have her here with me
There's not a thing I would change.

BLM

It still hurts.
I still drown in it if I let my thoughts linger
Watching the white people of the Western world learn
        about racism
Watching them get so angry
And feeling this sense of changing,

And then watching the trend pass.

I didn't go to protests –
Between anxiety and social anxiety and OCD,
        it wasn't an option for me
I beat myself up about it
A bit
Because they're not Really very good excuses-
Other people did it.
I didn't.

One of my friends turned out to be a racist.
'I mean, wasn't he a criminal?'

Like stealing is worthy of a death penalty
It makes me sick
I haven't spoken to him since.
Our mutual friends are still friends with him.
I try not to resent them for it.
They're all white, of course.
I ask them if they ever got through to him,
If the 'work' they were trying to do worked.
They sort of shrug.
They don't really know.
The thing about bigotry is that it's much nicer
    not to talk about it at all, actually.
That you can know someone's a good person, deep down.
It's much easier to know He is a good person,
    deep down, when you're white,
I imagine.
I hear he's doing great.
I get clumsy slivers of updates when our mutual friends
    forget to not mention him around me.
Black lives matter.
Kinda.
When it's trendy
When it's convenient

When there's nothing else to do
When you're incensed about it
When there's a hashtag
When you get to be the white person talking about
        'white people' because it lets you pretend
        that you are not also White People.
It's not very convincing
Not to me, at least.
BLM still hurts.
For everything I didn't do.
For everything it didn't do.
And black lives still matter
And they still kind of don't at all.

Creating

I started making earrings in the pandemic.
I started making a lot of things.
I always considered myself creative, if not artistic
More comfortable in words than colours,
Quicker to grab a pen than a pencil
Still halted by memories of Year 9 Art
Where I just couldn't seem to make things
        that were good enough.
My home is now filled with things that I made
I am the friend with a little bit of everything
Paint, ink sprays, polymer clay
Pyrography, texture paste, collaging stickers, washi tape
I got very into miniatures, of all things,
Careful small-scale attention
Creating and staging little rooms that hold as many
        stories as I care to write,
There are four in my bedroom,
There will be more with time.
I let myself cycle in and out of hobbies.
I made clothes in my last year of uni

And last Christmas
And I intend to make at least one skirt in these
        last dregs of summer.
I let myself drift in and out of things.
I let myself be bad at it
I let myself get better
I took up digital art,
I spend entire drawings complaining
        about the effort of it all
And proudly share them at the end.
I don't have to be anything
I can just create
There were months I didn't write a single poem
I remember the first crashing into my mind
        like a wave breaking,
Like I was gasping for air again.
There were months where I wrote a poem every day-
They were almost all bad, but that was okay.
I let myself play
Cast aside all the requirements and prerequisites
        and standards
Found beauty in the process again,

Took away the pressure of having something
>to show for it all in the end.

I have too many earrings now
Some of them I almost never wear.
But when I do,
I often get compliments
And I answer proudly
'Thanks, I made them.'

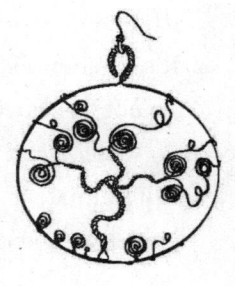

Post-pandemic

I think we're supposed to say it's over now,
I think it's supposed to be something that happened.
Concrete.
In the past.
I think it's supposed to be a tragedy that we
        lived through.
Things are supposed to be normal now,
We are supposed to be normal now.
No one asks about hugging any more
Very few people still wear masks
We don't worry about our grandparents in the same way
They're no longer vulnerable,
Just old now.
And there's privilege in that,
Right?
It's an able-bodied point of view
To not be scared any more.
So there's that.
My flatmate is a teacher now.
He tells me about the new students he sees

Children that grew up in it all,
Gaps grated into their education
And they are primed to slip through the holes.
And I find myself saying again, and again
That we have all been through a traumatic event.
That you can't just Back To Normal it away
That it impacts you, to spend so long feeling so unsafe,
That the isolation sits in you.
That very few of us had confronted death in that way,
In our squeaky clean oh-so developed nation
In our privilege of only sending soldiers to fight
        across the seas
It's been a long time since we've had to feel
So mortal.
And cost of living is taking food out of children's mouths
And so much is still happening now
That we can't just
Go back to new normal –
We need to feel
To process
To heal
To be able to sit with the reality and somehow make
        some kind of sense of it all,

If only internally.
Change happens, regardless.

But I implore you to sit with it,
If just for a second
To let yourself be
Overwhelmed
Heartbroken
Different
Changed
New
And then you can learn how this skin fits
How that feeling stretches as you move
    through this New Normal
Post-pandemic.